SPOTLIGHT ON NATIVE AMERICANS

IROQUOIS
(HAUDENOSAUNEE)

Wendell Rhodes

PowerKiDS
press

New York

Published in 2016 by The Rosen Publishing Group, Inc.
29 East 21st Street, New York, NY 10010

First Edition

Editor: Sarah Machajewski
Book Design: Samantha DeMartin
Reviewed by: Robert J. Conley, Former Sequoyah Distinguished Professor at Western Carolina University and Director of Native American Studies at Morningside College and Montana State University. Supplemental material reviewed by: Donald A. Grinde, Jr., Professor of Transnational/American Studies at the State University of New York at Buffalo.

Photo Credits: Cover MyLoupe/Universal Images Group/Getty Images; p. 5 Photo Researchers/ Science Source/Getty Images; pp. 6–7 Andoni Canela/age fotostock/Getty Images; pp. 8–9 Doug Lemke/Shutterstock.com; p. 11 bestofgreenscreen/Shutterstock.com; pp. 13, 16, 17, 19, 21, 23 Marilyn Angel Wynn/Nativestock/Getty Images; p. 14 Smithsonian Institution/Wikimedia Commons; p. 25 PhotoQuest/Archive Photos/Getty Images; p. 27 Stock Montage/Archive Photos/Getty Images; p. 29 Education Images/Universal Images Group/Getty Images.

Library of Congress Cataloging-in-Publication Data

Rhodes, Wendell.
   Iroquois (Haudenosaunee) / Wendell Rhodes.
      pages cm. — (Spotlight on Native Americans)
   Includes index.
   ISBN 978-1-5081-4150-1 (pbk.)
   ISBN 978-1-5081-4151-8 (6 pack)
   ISBN 978-1-5081-4153-2 (library binding)
   1. Iroquois Indians—History—Juvenile literature. 2. Iroquois Indians—Social life and customs—Juvenile literature. I. Title.
   E99.I7R494 2016
   974.7004'9755—dc23
                          2015036312

CONTENTS

AN INTRODUCTION TO THE HAUDENOSAUNEE

CHAPTER 1

The history of the people of North America dates back many years. **Ancestors** of Native Americans arrived on the continent thousands of years before recorded history. By the time Europeans arrived in the 16th century, Native American communities were thriving throughout North America. Today, there are more than 500 Native American groups in the United States and more than 600 groups in Canada.

The Haudenosaunee (hoh-dee-nuh-SHOH-nee) people, who were called the Iroquois (IHR-uh-kwoy) by Europeans, have had an important **role** in the history of Native Americans in North America. The Haudenosaunee **culture** is thought to date back to around the 1200s. By the 1600s, the Haudenosaunee people were known to Europeans as an important and powerful **confederacy**. Despite centuries of change, the Haudenosaunee people have been able to preserve their **heritage**. Today, they lead modern lives while also honoring the past.

The names "Haudenosaunee" and "Iroquois" are used to refer to people from six Native American nations—the Mohawks, Oneidas, Onondagas, Cayugas, Senecas, and Tuscaroras. Each of these peoples has a **unique** history and culture, but they're connected by cultural similarities, including language, beliefs, and traditions.

In this book, "Haudenosaunee" is used to speak generally about the communities that belong to the Six Nations. It's important to remember that each of the nations has a unique way of life, while together they share a set of customs, beliefs, and values.

MIGRATING TO NORTH AMERICA

CHAPTER 2

Traditionally, the Haudenosaunee people lived in present-day New York State. However, their ancestors weren't from there originally. One widely accepted theory states that ancestors of Native Americans traveled from eastern Asia to North America using a land bridge.

Earth went through an ice age many thousands of years ago. An ice age is a period of time marked by very cold temperatures. Most of Earth's water was frozen in great ice sheets, causing sea levels to be much lower than they are today. As a result, areas that are covered by water today were once dry. This was the case with the area between eastern Asia and Alaska. Ancestors of Native Americans may have used the land bridge to **migrate** between landmasses.

Many other theories also exist to explain how Native Americans came to live in North America. Some people feel the best way to describe this time in history is to think of it as ancient people coming from Asia, Africa, Europe, and the Pacific Islands, blending together before modern Europeans arrived, and forming cultures that were influenced by their new **environment**.

The way people think about this migration period is constantly changing as new discoveries are made. What is known, however, is that Native Americans' ancestors arrived from other continents more than 12,000 years ago.

INFLUENCED BY THE ENVIRONMENT

CHAPTER 3

As Earth's climate warmed, ancestors of Native Americans migrated down the continent and spread out. They settled in different areas and eventually lost contact with each other. Over time, these groups developed cultures that were based on their environment. The geography and climate influenced what kinds of homes they lived in, what they ate, and what they wore, and shaped other ways of life. Gradually, they adapted and modified their environment to meet their needs. This is called ecocentrism.

The Haudenosaunee may have settled in the area that's today New York State around the 1200s. This area is known as the Eastern Woodlands region. At the time, this hilly region was covered by woodlands. It had four seasons, including very cold winters. Deer and beaver were widespread.

The Haudenosaunee were not the only native people in this region. They were surrounded by Algonquian peoples, who were groups of Native Americans who spoke related languages. At this time, the Haudenosaunee were not a united group of nations. They fought each other and Algonquian-speaking peoples. War and violence were a part of everyday life, but some Haudenosaunee sought peace.

The Eastern Woodlands region provided plenty of water, wood from forests, plants, and animals that helped the Haudenosaunee survive.

PEACE AMONG THE HAUDENOSAUNEE

CHAPTER 4

Peace came to the Haudenosaunee by a Huron man named Deganawidah who lived with the Mohawk nation. Many people call him the Peacemaker. According to tradition, he was sent by the Creator to teach the laws of peace to the Haudenosaunee.

The Peacemaker used arrows to show the power of being united. He began by breaking a single arrow in half, which was easy. Then, he tied five arrows together. He couldn't break them. According to tradition, the Peacemaker said, "A single arrow is weak and easily broken. A bundle of arrows tied together cannot be broken. This represents the strength of having a confederacy."

Mohawk

Oneida

Onondaga

Cayuga

Seneca

Haudenosaunee territories 1600s

During the Peacemaker's journey, he met an Onondaga leader named Hayo'wetha. Hayo'wetha believed in the Peacemaker's message and wanted to unite the Haudenosaunee. However, Tadadaho, another Onondaga leader, stood in their way. Tadadaho was evil and feared by all. He was known to hate the message of peace. However, Hayo'wetha and the Peacemaker convinced him to accept by promising to give the Onondagas an important role in the new confederacy. The Mohawks, Oneidas, Cayugas, Senecas, and Onondagas became united under the Great Law of Peace, or Gayanesshagowa.

eastern white pine

The Peacemaker planted a tree in Onondaga territory, which was named the Great Tree of Peace. It symbolized the Great Law of Peace that guided Haudeonsaunee life from then on. The tree was an eastern white pine. The tree's bundle of five needles represents the five united Haudenosaunee nations.

THE GRAND COUNCIL
CHAPTER 5

Next, the Peacemaker took an arrow from each of the five nations. He bound them together, showing that the groups were united. The Peacemaker asked each nation to choose men to be their leaders. A leader is called a *hoyaneh*. Fifty leaders, or *hodiyahnehsonh (HOH-dee-yah-neh-sonh)*, formed the Grand Council. Every Haudenosaunee nation is represented on the Grand Council. The Tuscaroras, who joined the confederacy well after it was founded, are represented by the Oneidas.

Some people think the Grand Council was founded in 1142. Since then, it has been expected to make decisions based on the teachings of the Great Law of Peace. These principles help leaders solve problems and respect the Haudenosaunee people's basic rights.

The Great Law of Peace is considered to be one of the earliest examples of **democracy** in North America. Some people feel it influenced the United States' Founding Fathers, including Benjamin Franklin, who was familiar with it. Many principles of the Great Law of Peace can be seen in the U.S. Constitution. Today, the Haudeosaunee Grand Council is the oldest government in North America that still operates under the same principles as when it was founded.

Five arrows bound together is a symbol of unity for the Haudenosaunee nations.

NATION NAMES
CHAPTER 6

The name "Haudenosaunee" comes from the Iroquois language and means "people who build a house" or "people of the longhouse." This is the name the Haudenosaunee prefer to use. The name "Iroquois" comes from an Algonquian word that means "real snake," so many Haudenosaunee don't like to use it. The French called the Haudenosaunee the Iroquois Confederacy, and the English called them the Five Nations. When the Tuscaroras joined in the 1722, the confederacy became known as the Six Nations.

The Mohawk people, whose name means "People of the Flint" in the Iroquois language, are sometimes called Keepers of the Eastern Door. As the easternmost nation in upstate New York,

Grand Council of the Iroquois League

the Mohawks protected the confederacy's eastern border. The Senecas, who lived in western New York, are known as Keepers of the Western Door. They defended the Haudenosaunee's western border. They're also known as the "People of the Great Hill."

The name "Oneida" means "People of the Standing Stone," while the name "Cayuga" means "People of the Great Swamp." The Onondagas, whose name in Iroquois means "People of the Hills," are also called Keepers of the Central Fire because it's the capital of the Haudenosaunee Confederacy. The Grand Council gathers there, as promised by the Peacemaker.

Mohawk

Onondaga

Oneida

Seneca

Cayuga

Tuscarora

Haudenosaunee territories 1722

Each of the five original Haudenosaunee nations had a name that was based on the geography where they lived.

THE HAUDENOSAUNEE LONGHOUSE

CHAPTER 7

"Haudenosaunee" refers to the kind of houses used by the people in the Six Nations. Longhouses were commonly around 100 feet (30.5 m) long and around 20 feet (6.1 m) wide. They were built for large extended families, or clans, to live in.

Longhouses were made from materials found in the environment. The frame of a longhouse was made of saplings, or young trees. Cedar, hickory, and elm were commonly used. The frame was covered with **shingles** made of tree bark. The shingles were held down by rope made from natural fibers. The door was made of bark or animal skins.

longhouse interior

Longhouses didn't have windows, but they had smoke holes in the roof. The smoke holes were located above the fire pits inside the longhouse. The inside of a longhouse was divided by wooden screens, which separated families. There were raised platforms for sleeping, sitting, and storage, as well as cooking areas.

The Haudenosaunee people lived in villages. In the 1600s, there may have been between 200 and 3,000 people in a village. The villages were usually settled near forests and freshwater sources. Water was necessary for survival, and forests provided protection, food, and materials for building.

Without the modern conveniences we have today, the Haudenosaunee had to make use of the resources and land around them. Longhouses were built using trees from the forests near villages. When there were no longer trees to use, villages moved elsewhere.

HAUDENOSAUNEE SOCIETY

CHAPTER 8

Haudenosaunee society is organized into clans. The Haudenosaunee nations are matrilineal, which means clan membership is traced through the mother's side. Clans are named after animals, such as wolf, bear, and turtle. People who belong to the same clan can belong to different nations. For example, a person in the Mohawk wolf clan is related to a person in the Oneida wolf clan.

Women are very powerful in Haudenosaunee society. Each clan is led by a clan mother. In the past, this was the oldest woman in the clan. The clan mother is responsible for making decisions, which in the past included choosing the *hoyaneh* to represent the clan in the Grand Council.

In the past, the Haudenosaunee were farmers. Men helped clear fields for farming. Women planted squash, corn, and beans, which were known as the three sisters. These crops grew well in the Haudenosaunee's lands. Women also gathered food such as mushrooms and berries from the nearby woodlands.

Men were hunters and most commonly hunted deer, which were **abundant** in their environment. They also fished using nets, hooks, and lines. Haudenosaunee men hunted using arrows and spears made from flint. They attached the arrowheads to handles made of wood or bone.

The Haudenosaunee diet was based on food that was easily found in their environment. However, many of the animals and plants they ate were hard to come by in the cold winter months. To prepare for this, the Haudenosaunee dried and stored food inside their longhouse. This was one way of handling the challenges of their environment.

CLOTHING AND WAMPUM BELTS

CHAPTER 9

Like their housing and food, the Haudenosaunee's clothing was made from resources in their environment. Clothing was made from animal skins and fur. Men wore **breechcloths** and leggings. Women wore skirts, **tunics**, and leggings. Moccasins were made of animal skin, but could be made of cornhusks, too. The way clothing was decorated using beads, feathers, or dyes was different for each clan and nation.

Wampum was a well-known part of Haudenosaunee culture. Wampum are beads made of clam shells. The Narragansett and Wampanoag people originally made them. Hayo'wetha introduced wampum to the Haudenosaunee culture.

In the past, the Haudenosaunee people traded fur and crops for wampum, which were very valuable. Wampum were woven together to make belts, but the belts were never worn as clothing. They were used in ceremonies and were designed to record laws and Haudenosaunee history.

Many wampum had religious meaning, and wampum belts were present at important political gatherings.

The Haudenosaunee didn't use wampum as money or for trade with Europeans as other Native American groups did. However, they did exchange wampum belts with Europeans to recognize peace treaties. One of the most famous wampum belts is the Hiawatha belt. It represents the unity of the five original Haudenosaunee nations.

The flag used by the Six Nations features the design that's on the Hiawatha wampum belt. The four white squares represent the Senecas, Oneidas, Cayugas, and Mohawks. The white pine tree in the center stands for the Onondagas. The squares are linked to the pine tree, representing the nations' unity.

TRADITIONAL CEREMONIES AND BELIEFS

CHAPTER 10

Haudenosaunee culture is rich with traditions and beliefs that have guided the people of the Six Nations for centuries. Many **versions** of the Haudenosaunee's **creation story** say that Earth was created by water animals, a **celestial** being named Sky Woman, and her twin grandsons. The creation story explains how their people came to live and survive in their environment.

Traditionally, the Haudenosaunee followed a calendar that had 13 months and 13 moons. Many traditional ceremonies are based on the changing of the seasons. This includes the Thunder Festival in April, the Green Corn Festival in August or September, and the Harvest Festival in October. Every ceremony or important gathering begins and ends with the Gano:nyok, which are words that give thanks for the important things in Haudenosaunee life.

Ceremonies are a way for the Haudenosaunee people to give thanks to the environment for the resources it has provided. They're ready to acknowledge the important role nature played in their lives, especially corn and deer, which had countless uses. Though the Haudenosaunee people of today don't rely on nature's resources as much as their ancestors, those resources are still greatly respected.

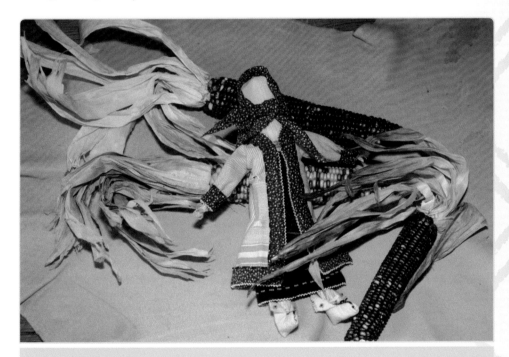

Corn was extremely important to the Haudenosaunee, as well as other Native American communities, which is why it's honored through ceremony. The Haudenosaunee used corn for food and to make important objects. Cornhusk dolls were used to teach children important values. For example, the dolls have no face, which teaches that beauty is not important and that all people are the same.

CHANGE COMES QUICKLY
CHAPTER 11

The Haudenosaunee lived a largely undisturbed life until the 1500s, when they first came into contact with Europeans. When European fur traders passed through Haudenosaunee lands, they found an organized confederacy of nations.

At first, the Haudenosaunee's relationship with Europeans was based on trade. Beaver fur was in high demand in Europe, and the Haudenosaunee knew how to trap the animal that was so abundant in their lands. They traded beaver pelts with Dutch, French, and English traders for knives, cooking tools, cloth, scissors, and weapons.

These tools changed the Haudenosaunee's ways of life. They no longer had to rely only on resources taken from their environment. Because of their new weapons and tools, the Haudenosaunee nations grew very powerful and were able to expand their territory. In some cases, European influence affected how the Haudenosaunee dressed and the style of houses in which they lived.

During the 1600s, European nations began colonizing land in North America, including the territory of the Five Nations. The Haudenosaunee had a good relationship with the Dutch and English at first, but had a strained relationship with the French. During the **French and Indian War**, the Haudenosaunee Confederacy sided with the English and helped them win.

The Haudenosaunee nations sided with the English during the wars of the 1700s because they often had a poor relationship with the French.

DURING AND AFTER THE WAR

CHAPTER 12

After the French and Indian War, colonists continued settling on Haudenosaunee lands. In 1768, leaders from the Six Nations met with English leaders at Fort Stanwix in New York to establish boundaries between Native American land and English land. However, colonists disrespected this agreement and settled on Haudenosaunee land anyway.

When the American Revolution began in 1775, both American colonists and the British pressured the Six Nations to support their cause. The Grand Council tried to remain **neutral**, but this didn't last long, and the confederacy soon split. The Oneidas and Tuscaroras supported the American cause, while the Senecas, Cayugas, Onondagas, and Mohawks supported the English. Notably, a Mohawk man named Joseph Brant led violent attacks against colonists and other Haudenosaunee nations. Throughout the American Revolution, the Six

Nations that were once united fought each other for people who would later not be so kind to them.

In 1784, the Haudenosaunee Confederacy signed a treaty with the new United States that forced them to give up much of their land. Eventually, the United States forced the Haudenosaunee onto **reservations**, and their ways of life changed greatly.

Life on reservations was completely different from the way the Haudenosaunee had lived for centuries. In the end, many parts of their lives changed because of the decisions the U.S. government made for them.

LIFE TODAY

CHAPTER 13

Over the last several centuries, the Haudenosaunee, as well as other Native American groups, faced many challenges as they tried to survive in a changing world. The Haudenosaunee have been able to adapt to new ways of life while also holding on to their rich cultural traditions. Today, people of Haudenosaunee descent live around the world. They are educators, doctors, lawyers, businesspeople, and more. However, life on reservations is commonly hard, with many of the residents living in poverty and struggling with problems such as drug and alcohol addiction and **obesity**.

Many Haudenosaunee are committed to preserving their heritage by teaching young generations and nonnatives about traditional Haudenosaunee culture. One of the ways in which the past has been truly preserved is through efforts to keep the confederacy strong. The Grand Council still meets today as it did in the past. Since 1924, leaders of the Six Nations have been elected by the people. Leaders make decisions in the best interest of the Haudenosaunee people and oversee efforts to bring economic, social, and cultural success to them.

Each of the nations in the Haudenosaunee Confederacy has a unique identity, but together, they form a strong partnership that's committed to preserving the past and building a successful future.

A Mohawk chief presents several examples of wampum belts. This picture was taken in 2012.

GLOSSARY

abundant: Available in large amounts.

ancestor: Someone who comes before others in their family tree.

breechcloth: A piece of clothing that's worn around the waist.

celestial: Having to do with the heavens.

confederacy: An alliance, or partnership, of nations.

creation story: A story that explains how the world and its people came into existence.

culture: The beliefs and ways of life of a group of people.

democracy: A system of government whose leaders are elected by the people.

environment: The surroundings in which a person, animal, or plant lives.

French and Indian War: From 1754 to 1763, a war between the British and French over territory in North America.

heritage: Traditions that have been passed down from older generations.

migrate: To move from one area to another.

neutral: Not taking sides.

obesity: The medical condition of being severely overweight.

reservation: Land set aside by the government for a specific Native American group or groups to live on.

role: The part something plays.

shingle: A small, thin piece of building material laid in overlapping rows on the roof or outer walls.

tunic: A loose piece of clothing that's worn over the body and that reaches the knees.

unique: Special or different.

version: A form of something that is slightly different from other forms of the same type of thing.

FOR MORE INFORMATION

BOOKS

Dolbear, Emily J., and Peter Benoit. *The Iroquois*. New York, NY: Children's Press, 2011.

Johnson, Michael G. *Iroquois: People of the Longhouse*. Richmond Hill, ON, Canada: Firefly Books, 2013.

Smith-Llera, Danielle. *The Iroquois: The Past and Present of the Haudenosaunee*. North Mankato, MN: Capstone Press, 2016.

WEBSITES

Due to the changing nature of Internet links, PowerKids Press has developed an online list of websites related to the subject of this book. This site is updated regularly. Please use this link to access the list: www.powerkidslinks.com/sona/haud

INDEX